East Wickham and Welling

Peter J. Tester, F.S.A.
Vice-President of the
Kent Archaeological Society

Acknowledgments
I would like to acknowledge the help of the
Local Studies Centre of the
Bexley Libraries and Museums Department,
and to the Kent Archaeological Society for
permission to reproduce illustrations from
Archaeologia Cantiana.

Peter Tester

Directorate of Education
LIBRARIES & MUSEUMS DEPARTMENT

Bexley
LONDON BOROUGH

Cover: High Street, Welling, looking eastwards from near the Nag's Head, *c*1910.

1991 2nd edition by P J Tester.

ISBN 0-902541-28-5.

No part of any publication may be reproduced, stored in a retrieval system, or transmitted in any form or by any means, electronic, photocopying, recording, or otherwise, without the prior permission of the Chief Librarian.

Contents

Origins	5
Watling Street	6
Roman Burials	9
The evidence of place-names	10
The Medieval Church and Manor	12
The Leighs of Addington and East Wickham	18
Sir John Hawkins and the East Wickham Tithes	20
The Payne Family of Welling	22
Payne's Charity	24
Danson	26
The Eighteenth Century	27
The Highways	30
The Nineteenth Century	34
Suburbia triumphant	40
References	46
Index	49

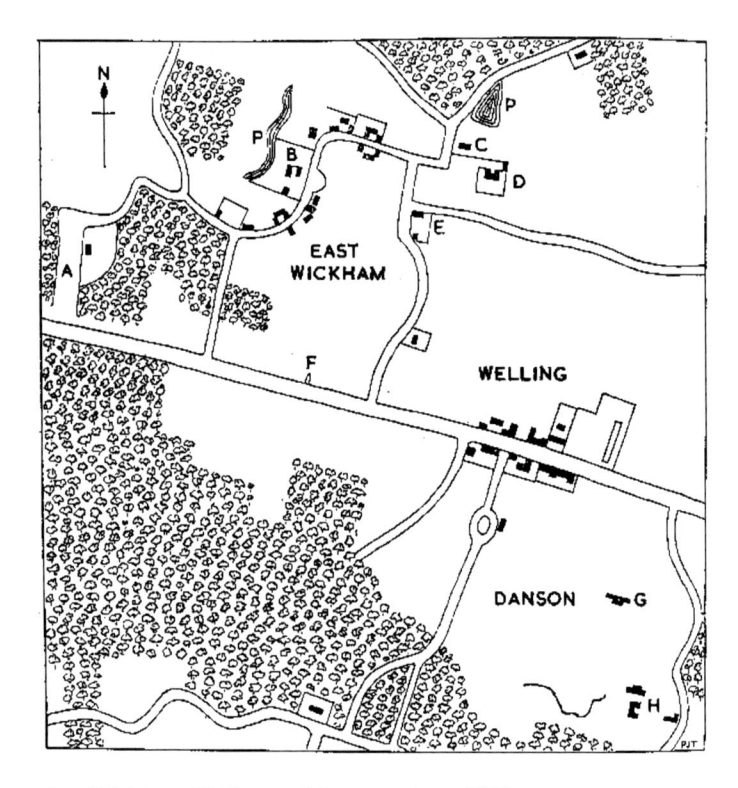

East Wickham, Welling and Danson, about 1769.
Redrawn and adapted from the map by Andrews, Dury and Herbert.
A *Shoulder of Mutton Green.* **B** *East Wickham House.*
C *St. Michael's Church.* **D** *Sir John Olyffe's House.*
E *Foster's School.* **F** *Tenth Milestone from London.*
G *Danson Mansion* **H** *Old Manor House of Danson.* **PP** *Ponds.*

Origins

Within living memory, East Wickham and Welling were little more than two separate hamlets closely related to the main road between Dover and London and about ten miles from the latter.
Their origin and history were linked with this highway which was first constructed by the Romans and has never ceased to serve as one of the most important routes in the country.

A map of 1769 shows Welling as merely two rows of dwellings facing each other across the road where the High Street is now, extending eastward for about two hundred yards from the approximate position of the modern Nag's Head public house. East Wickham appears as a less compact straggle of buildings north of the highway, lying on a track branching off at Shoulder of Mutton Green and winding north-eastward, roughly on the course of the existing Wickham Street, to join Wickham Lane a short distance south of the old church of St. Michael[1].
Both settlements are shown on one of the earliest maps of Kent, dating from 1572 where Welling appears as *Wellingstret*[2].
Until the nineteenth century East Wickham was included in the parish of Plumstead, as was the north side of Welling. The area south of the Dover Road was in the parish of Bexley, including the Danson estate then extending up to the hamlet of Welling and entered by a gate at the present junction of the High Street and Danson Crescent. North of the road lay open farmland with the wooded slopes of Shooters Hill to the west and the open waste of Bexley Heath to the east, which was not enclosed and settled until 1819-20.

Watling Street

The earliest trace of human activity in this area is a neolithic stone axe-head found about 1910 on land belonging to East Wickham (Gibson's) Farm, and is probably not less than four thousand years old.[3] It may, however, be no more than a stray find and does not necessarily indicate a permanent settlement at that remote period. In 1986 some sherds of Bronze Age pottery were discovered on the site of Hook Lane School (*Kent Archaeological Review*, No. 92). In a sense, the main road itself constitutes the most important ancient monument in the locality, originating in the second half of the first century soon after the conquest of south-east Britain following the Roman invasion of A.D.43. It formed part of a route running diagonally across the country from the Kent coast, through London and on to Chester, and was later known as Watling Street. This name can be traced back as far as the ninth century and is Old English in origin; what it was called in Roman times is unknown. An early form of the name was *waeclingastraet*, the first element of which is identical with an old name for St. Albans, so that 'Watling Street' may have been first applied to the route between that place and London.[4] Later its meaning was extended to apply to the whole of its course, including the part running through Kent.

A charter of A.D. 814 refers to the highway from the foot of Shooters Hill to Crayford as *casincgstraet*[5] and it seems always to have run in a straight course between those two points, as was characteristic of Roman roads, so we may assume that it coincided closely with the present highway, the A207.

No identifiable remains of Roman road-construction have been found in Welling, but this is not surprising as such roads often took the form of a bank, or *agger*, of loose stones and gravel, and in post-Roman times would become obliterated by constant use and lack of repair. Traces of the *agger* have been observed east of Dartford where it is recorded to have been twenty-four feet wide and between two and three feet high[6] At

Dartford in 1898 the paving of the Roman ford through the River Darent was found beneath the modern road, and some of the stones were re-set near a pathway in the Public Gardens behind Dartford Central Library.[7]

South-eastward the road continued from Welling across Bexley Heath, through Crayford, Dartford, Rochester, and on to Canterbury where in Roman times it threw off four branches: to Reculver (*Regulbium*), Richborough (*Rutupiae*), Dover (*Dubris*), and Lympne (*Lemanis*). Canterbury (*Durovernum*) was then the cantonal capital of the Kentish people, and through it would pass all the traffic coming from the Continent to any of the four coastal places mentioned and proceeding to London (*Londinium*). In later centuries the importance of Dover was maintained while the other branches of the route declined into insignificance, and for this reason the main course through Kent became known as the Dover Road.

A Roman travellers' guide, the *Antonine Itinerary*, noted the existence of a place called *Noviomagus* on the route ten miles out of London, and this has led to a belief that it may have been located at Welling. The matter has been a subject of debate in antiquarian circles for a long time, and at present the evidence is interpreted in favour of *Noviomagus* having been at Crayford, as indicated on the current Ordnance Survey Map of Roman Britain.[8]

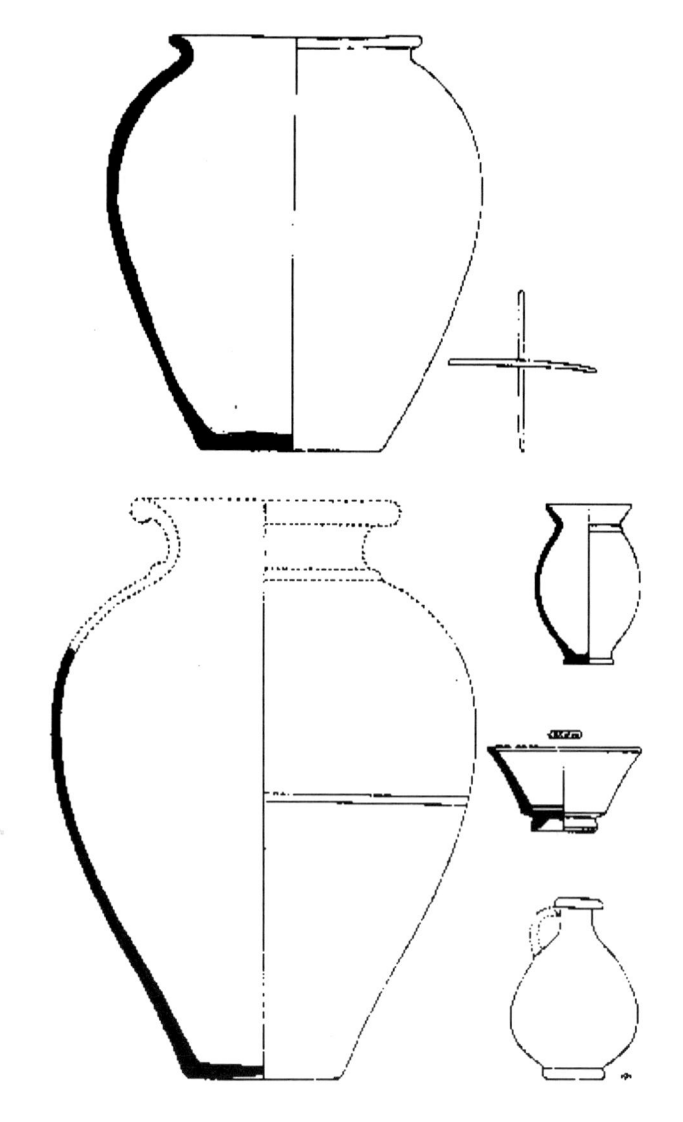

*Roman pottery from Welling. Top: Cinerary urn with a cross impressed on the base.
Found about 250 yards north of the High Street at the east end of the hamlet in 1842.
Below: Urn with three small accompanying vessels, found on the south side of the High Street when it was widened in 1938.
(Reproduced by permission of the Editor of Archaeologia Cantiana.)
In 1989 a further quantity of pottery was discovered by members of the Kent Archaeological Rescue Unit on a site on the south side of the High Street close to the Guy Earl of Warwick. A report is in process of preparation.*

Roman burials

From time to time Roman burials have come to light at Welling although there are no records of foundations or other traces of buildings of that age in association. In 1829 a Roman urn was found south of the road at the western end of the hamlet, and in 1842 another containing cremated human remains was dug up in a field on the opposite side and to the east. When the High Street was being widened in 1938, a group of Roman pottery vessels was found about two hundred yards north-west of the modern Guy Earl of Warwick public house, comprising three urns, the most complete of which contained cremated bones and three smaller vessels presumably holding offerings of food and drink to the spirit of the dead person. There was a jug, a beaker and a red samian ware cup with the name of the Gaulish potter, Celsus, stamped inside the base. He is known to have been working about A.D. 120-5, and this provides a useful indication of the age of the burials.[9]

The fact that these discoveries, although not closely grouped, all fall roughly within the limits of the later hamlet raises the question as to whether there was a small settlement here on the roadside as early as Roman times. In support of this it has been observed that the field next to that in which the urn was found in 1842 had produced Roman coins.

At the junction of Wickham Lane and King's Highway a Roman lead sarcophagus with indications of a wooden lining was found in 1887, four feet deep, containing the skeleton of a young girl, and near by were traces of a second burial. The sarcophagus was temporarily deposited in Plumstead mortuary and later given burial in the cemetary by the vicar who acted in this respect, according to a contemporary account, 'in defiance of all right, all reason and much remonstrance'. It was subsequently disinterred through the efforts of the Kentish antiquary, George Payne, and is now in Maidstone Museum.[10] From the mode of burial it may be assumed that the girl was of some social standing and it is likely that her home was not far distant. The valley running from East Wickham towards the Thames would indeed have provided a suitable site for a Roman villa.

The evidence of place-names

No archaeological remains have come from East Wickham or Welling to prove that they were settlements in Anglo-Saxon times, but the place-name evidence is important in this respect and must be considered in detail. We can dispose at once of the fallacy that Welling was called 'Well End' because travellers who had survived the dangers of Shooters Hill considered that they had made a fortunate termination of the most hazardous stage of their journey when they passed through the hamlet. The place was called *wellyngs* as long ago as 1362,[11] and it is generally agreed that the first element comes from the Old English *wella* meaning a well or spring. Springs do in fact occur hereabouts, one being the source of a rivulet feeding Danson Lake. The significance of the suffix *ing* is, however, more problematical; it is a common ending in English place-names and was in many cases originally *ingas*, signifying at first the people who lived there and later the place where they lived. Until recently *ingas* names were thought to relate to the earliest phase of the English settlement in the fifth and sixth centuries, but this is now disputed and it may be that names with the suffix *ham*, as in 'Wickham', should occupy that chronological position.[12] In its singular form *ing* the element could mean simply 'place', but to complicate the matter early singular endings were later occasionally changed to plurals.[13]

As we have no very early pre-Conquest forms of the name Welling, the terminal 's' in 1362 may be misleading. Although place-name study is dangerous ground for all but the expert, it may be tentatively suggested that in the present case 'Welling' means simply 'the place of the spring', rather than indicating an early Anglo-Saxon settlement. Moreover, such settlements were not usually on the direct course of a Roman road, the newcomers generally preferring to make their homes a short distance from the highway, as apparently in the case of East Wickham.

The form *Estwycham* occurs as early as 1284.[14] As at West Wickham, the old settlement lay not far from a

Roman road and it has been noted that out of twenty-nine place-names in which the Old English compound *wicham* occurs, twenty-five are on or near Roman highways,[15] although the signifance of this relationship is still a matter for speculation. The name means a dwelling place or settlement.[16] Having regard to the recently revised dating of place-names ending in *ham*, and also the topography of the site, situated at the head of a valley running into the Thames, and near a Roman road, there exists a strong possibility that East Wickham originated as a farmstead created in an early phase of the Anglo-Saxon settlement.

The medieval church and manor

There is a scarcity of revealing information about either place in the Middle Ages. Domesday Book, in 1086, mentions neither by name, East Wickham being included without separate identification in the entry for *Plumstede*, then held by the abbot of St. Augustine's Abbey, Canterbury, and the area south of the road being part of *Bix* (Bexley) which was the property of the archbishop.

The oldest surviving building is St. Michael's church, standing on the brow of a steep hill where Wickham Lane dips down towards Plumstead, and it dates from the early thirteenth century, with some later alterations. Apparently it was built as a chapel for the manor rather than a parish church and its plan is a simple rectangle without structural division between nave and chancel. The walls were originally of flint

The old St. Michael's Church, East Wickham, as it appeared in the 19th century. The porch shown was later replaced by a vestry.

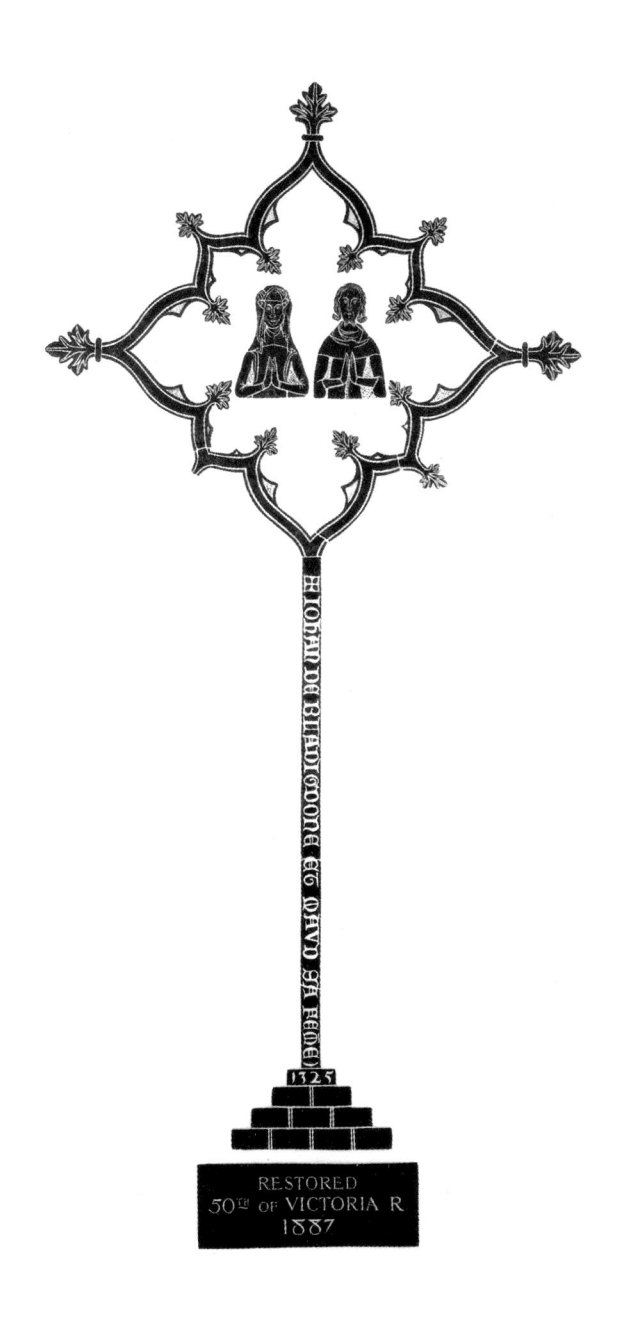

*Brass in East Wickham Church to John and
Maud de Bladigdone. The date 1325 is a modern insertion and
may not be strictly accurate.*

and the earliest details are two thirteenth-century lancet windows in the north wall, and the south doorway now covered by a modern vestry replacing the earlier porch. Square-framed Perpendicular windows were inserted in the fifteenth century and there has been much rebuilding and patching in more recent times in stone and brick.[17] In 1969 the building was transferred to the ownership of the Greek Orthodox Church and some of its fittings have been removed to the new Anglican church near by. Among these is the fourteenth-century brass to John de Bladigdone and his wife Maud, the half-effigies of whom are enclosed in an open floriated cross with the French inscription remaining on the shaft. This is now mounted on wood and displayed in the north aisle of the new church.

The stone from which it was lately removed was not its original setting for it had been lifted in the nineteenth century from its medieval slab, still lying in the middle of the church, and re-set on a new stone near the altar. A careful examination of the brass shows that some of the cross is Victorian replacement (1887) though the effigies are unrestored. By comparison with the indent, or recess made for the reception of the brass in its medieval Purbeck marble slab, it is possible to observe that the restoration was slightly defective. The distance between the lateral extremities of the cross should be nearly four inches greater than in its restored form, and the floriated terminations should be more angular, like those on a similar cross-brass in the church at Stone, near Dartford. Never-the-less, the brass is remarkable in that the male effigy is among the the earliest representations on a brass in this country of a man in civilian costume. John is shown with shoulder-length hair and a forked beard. He wears a tight-sleeved tunic, his forearms appearing through openings in the sleeves of an outer supertunic, or cotehardie, buttoned down the front. Over his shoulders is a cape with an attached hood. Maud wears a close-sleeved kirtle under a sleeveless surcoat open at the sides to waist level. Over her head is a veil and her hair is arranged in a braid over each ear, while her throat and chin are covered by a wimple. The costume is firm evidence for the fourteen-century age of the brass although the date 1325 now appearing in arabic numerals is a Victorian insertion and may be only approximately accurate.[18]

Bladigdone, or *Bladindon*, was the medieval name for the modern Blendon, lying in those days well inside the parish of Bexley, and it is therefore curious that John de Bladigdone was not buried in St. Mary's church in Bexley village.

Until 1845 the interior of this little church possessed a remarkable series of medieval mural paintings, once no doubt covering the walls on all sides and of which some traces still remain. On the north wall can still be made out the figure of the patron saint, St. Michael, weighing souls, a popular medieval subject, and on either side of the east window are earlier paintings, the southern figures seeming to depict the risen Christ with Mary Magdalene kneeling before him. At one time the whole of the north wall had similar paintings, as described on the eve of their destruction, the identifiable subjects including: the Visitation of Mary to Elizabeth, Christ before the High Priest, Christ and Nicodemus, St. Michael contending with Satan for the body of Moses, Angels appearing to the Shepherds, the Flight into Egypt, Herod enquiring of the Three Kings, and the Holy Family. These were all judged on stylistic grounds to belong to the thirteenth century and their destruction due to the disinterest of all in authority, despite urgent protests by the British Archaeological Association and others, was undoubtedly an artistic tragedy.

Apparently the destruction was occasioned by the desire of the local churchwarden and squire, Richard Jones, to create a suitable setting on the north wall for a memorial tablet to his late wife.[19]

A low recess in the south wall is all that remains of a medieval priest's door, the upper part having been destroyed in later re-building. Some stones found built into the walls during restoration in 1926 bear twelfth-century carving and have been mistakenly interpreted as indicating that the church itself is of that age, whereas they are more likely to be re-used material from an earlier building, not necessarily on the same site. At the east end are traces of the original triplet of lancet windows partly destroyed when the existing late-medieval window was inserted.

Churches dedicated to St. Michael were frequently built on elevated sites in accordance with the medieval concept of the archangel hovering high above the earth. An obvious and striking example is St. Michael's Mount off the Cornish coast. It is therefore significant that East Wickham church stands at the summit of a steep slope, as can be best appreciated by viewing it from below the junction of Wickham Lane and Lodge Hill.

An important feature of medieval church life was the undertaking of pilgrimages, and if any route in England deserves to be called 'The Pilgrims' Way' it is surely the London-to-Dover Road passing through Welling on its way to Canterbury. Following the murder there in 1170 of Archbishop Thomas Becket, his shrine was visited until the Reformation by great numbers of pilgrims journeying *the hooly blisful martir for to seke* as Chaucer expressed it. Like the pilgrims in his *Canterbury Tales*, they rode from London along the old road over Shooters Hill and through Welling, stopping at inns along the way for lodging and refreshment. Their mood was often that of holiday makers rather than penitents and, as Chaucer shows, they were drawn from all ranks of society. For three and a half centuries the inhabitants of Welling would have seen parties of them in spring and summer pass through or perhaps halt to water their horses at a roadside pond, or refresh themselves at a local hostelry.

Other travellers of a different kind passed the same way: in 1381 the Kentish rebels of the Peasants' Revolt made their riotous way to London gathering support from the areas along their route, intent on forcing the king and his ministers to redress their grievances. A generation later, in 1415, Henry V and his army returned this way from the victory at Agincourt and the sight must have drawn workers in the fields bordering Welling to the roadside to watch them pass. But quite apart from these dramatic occasions, Welling would have seen a constant flow of day-to-day traffic; farm carts and riders on horseback, merchants and travellers on foot, and the occasional great lady borne on a litter, all on their way to or from the capital.

The names of two of the medieval lords of the manor of East Wickham have been commemorated in local street names on the modern council estate. Burnell Avenue recalls Robert Burnell who died in 1292 and was Bishop of Bath and Wells, and also Lord Chancellor from 1274 until his death. He has been described as a covetous and ambitious man who gathered estates in nineteen counties including eighty-two manors, of which East Wickham was one. He was the trusted minister of Edward I whom he accompanied to France when Prince of Wales in 1260, and ten years later the king endeavoured unsuccessfuly to have him created Archbishop of Canterbury.[20] After his death his estates went to a nephew and later descended to Sir William Lovell whose grandson, Francis, was créated a viscount and Knight of the Garter in 1483 by Richard III after whose death two years later, and in the reign of Henry VII, Lovell joined the supporters of the imposter and rebel, Lambert Simnel. Upon the collapse of the rebellion he seems to have taken refuge in his own house where he starved to death.[21] His association with East Wickham is celebrated in the name of Lovel Avenue.

The Leighs of Addington and East Wickham

In 1562 the manorial rights of East Wickham were purchased for £400 by Sir John Olyffe of Foxgrave in Kent,[22] alderman of London and member of the Merchant Taylors company. On his death the property descended to his daughter and heiress, Joan, who married Francis Leigh of Addington in Surrey. Their eldest son was named Olyffe (or Olif) in honour of the union of the two families and he inherited East Wickham after his father's death in 1576. Sir Olyffe received in 1610 a licence to impark five hundred acres of land there and in the manor of Bexley, and during the early part of the reign of James I he was Keeper of the Great Park at Eltham, a remunerative office which he sold in 1610 for the considerable sum of £1,200.[23] Among his local business transactions he purchased in 1609 forty acres of woodland known as Belgrove on the south side of the Dover Road and in the manor of Bexley, together with several other acres of wood and pasture. This opened the way for the Leigh family to become eventually the squires of Bexley, a position they held for successive generations until the nineteenth century.[24] The part of the main road from Welling Corner to beyond the railway bridge is known to this day as Bellegrove from its association with the wood called by that name in the seventeenth century.

Charles Leigh, brother of Sir Olyffe, was of an adventurous disposition and in 1597 he set sail from Gravesend with two ships on a voyage across the Atlantic, ostensibly for purposes of trade and fishing, but also intending to rob any Spanish ships they might encounter. They reached the Gulf of St. Lawrence where he had an unsuccessful engagement with four French vessels. One of his ships was wrecked off Cape Breton but he rescued the crew and proceeded to Newfoundland. There he captured a valuable Breton ship (he apparently regarded all foreign vessels as his lawful prey) and in this he returned to England, arriving in the Thames a month later and claiming the vessel as a prize.

Another voyage was commenced in 1603 when he sailed from Woolwich for Guiana and reached the north coast of South America two months later. Here he traded with the natives and searched unsuccessfully for gold. Sickness overwhelmed the little colony he tried to establish and supplies had to be sent out by his brother, Olyffe, but Charles died on board his ship while preparing to return home, leaving a son, Olyffe, who is recorded to have been baptised at Addington in 1597.[25]

Addington was, in fact, the family seat of the Leighs and to what extent they were resident in East Wickham is not clear. It is probable that when they lived there they occupied a house a short distance south-east of the church, described by Hasted towards the end of the eighteenth century as 'an ancient good looking seat lately pulled down', and he suggested that it had been built by Sir John Olyffe in the reign of Elizabeth I.[26] When the site for the new church was being prepared in 1932, some foundations were uncovered which may well have belonged to this house. On the wall of the old church there is a memorial to Catherine, wife of John Leigh, who died in 1715, indicating that the family still had direct connections with the place at that time, and they retained possession until 1737. Through a union of the Leigh and Goldie families some property at Bostall Heath became known as Goldie-Leigh, still surviving in the name of the hospital there at the present time. The Leighs also had property at Hawley, near Dartford, where a terrace of brick cottages on the main road bears their name.

Sir John Olyffe is remembered in East Wickham by the modern street-name of Olyffe Avenue, and the Leighs by Leigh Place.

Sir John Hawkins and the East Wickham Tithes

An Elizabethan adventurer of much the same spirit as Charles Leigh, but rather more successful in his enterprises, was Captain (later Sir) John Hawkins. He was concerned in improving the design and building of ships, at that time carried on in the naval dockyards of Woolwich and Deptford. This association may have been responsible for his interest in the neighbouring locality of East Wickham for in 1574 he obtained possession of the tithes for the purpose of founding an almshouse for the relief and support of poor seamen and shipwrights, a project realised in 1592 at Chatham where the institution still exists. The constitution provided for the care of twelve inmates who each received two shillings weekly for their support.[27] In the

Iron-bound chest formerly in the old St. Michael's Church. It probably dates from the 17th century, but the local belief that it came from the Spanish Armada and was given to the church by Sir John Hawkins has no historical support.

Middle Ages tithes had been collected from inhabitants of parishes for the purpose of maintaining the clergy and dispensing charity, but at the Reformation so much ecclesiastical property was confiscated, including that of the monasteries, that tithes in many instances came into the hands of laymen who might be disposed to use them for charitable purposes.

On Shooters Hill in 1588 a beacon was prepared to signal the approach of the Spanish Armada. Many years previously William Lambarde had published a map of the Kentish beacons and this reveals how the warning lights would have passed from hilltop to hilltop from the south coast northward to Shooters Hill through a gap in the North Downs in the lower Medway area.[28]

The Shooters Hill beacon would have given the warning to London and also to a wide area of north-west Kent. While the inhabitants of East Wickham and Welling turned anxious eyes towards the hill, Hawkins was commanding the rear squadron of the English fleet following the Armada up the Channel, and he was knighted for his part in an action off the Isle of Wight. A less creditable side of his activities was his involvement in the trade in African slaves for whom he apparently felt none of the compassion he displayed for poor seamen of his own race. On his coat of arms there was depicted the figure of a bound and captive Moor in reference to one of Hawkin's victories. He left £50 to the poor of Deptford where he maintained his residence, and equal amounts to both London and Plymouth.[29]

The Payne family of Welling

A name that occurs frequently in wills and leases of the sixteenth and seventeenth centuries is that of the Payne family who possessed houses and land in and around Welling. In 1527 there is reference to John and Thomas Payne in the will of John Clerke of Bexley and bequests are made there to William the son of Henry Payne. A brass in St. Michael's church commemorates William Payn, Yeoman of the Guard, who died in 1568, and his wives Elizabeth, Joan and Joan. He is depicted wearing his Yeoman's uniform with a crowned Tudor rose on the chest, very similar to that worn today by the Yeomen of the Guard on ceremonial occasions. The

Brass in East Wickham Church, to William Payn, Yeoman of the Guard, with his wives (one missing) and three sons, 1568.

figure of one of the wives is missing and there are diminutive effigies of their three children placed below. When the brass was removed to be remounted in the new church it was found that the reverse side of the inscription bore the Latin epitaph of John Auncell who died in 1511 and is described as 'a monk (*monachus*) of this place', referring to some unidentified monastery, the plate having obviously been taken from a religious house dissolved in the time of Henry VIII.[30]

John Payne, whose will was proved in 1589, founded a local charity of which fuller particulars will be given below.

In 1603 there died Edward and Elizabeth Payne 'of Wellinge' who 'departed this life together' on the twentieth of November. They were buried in Bexley churchyard and a note in the register shows that they were victims of the plague then prevalent in London. The same register records that on the sixth of January 1604 another plague victim was buried, James Richmond, a servant of William Payne. It is not difficult to appreciate how the plague spread from London to Welling considering it stood on a main highway only ten miles from the City, with travellers constantly passing through or resting there on their journey.

The Payne family tomb stands under the yew tree in St. Mary's churchyard in Bexley village and bears also the names of William, son of Edward and Elizabeth Payne(d.1627) and his wife Jane(d.1666), also their son, Ephraim (d.1677). On the side of the weathered brick tomb is a small modern tablet recording that the ashes of the last male member of the family, James Vernon Payne, were enclosed there in 1951, and there is also an inscription to Betty Johnson, daughter of Edith Nodder (née Payne) who died in 1982.

Ephraim Payne, mentioned above, is referred to in 1632 as a citizen and Clothworker of London and his father, William, as a yeoman. Ephraim's son, George, was in 1684 described as a Skinner and citizen of London.

Payne's charity

John Payne, yeoman of East Wickham, left in his will in 1589 both his houses in Welling to his wife Katherine who was to possess them until her death, after which they were to go to John Nate and his heirs. But if his issue failed, the house then let to John Jude should be used for the relief of the poor. His other house, then occupied by John Walton, was left to William Payne, son of Edward Payne, on condition that he maintained the fences between the two properties and that the poor should never be burdened with that expense.

In 1677 an inquest was held at Eltham to enquire into the abuse of charities and it was found that the descendants of John Nate had died out long ago. The commissioners therefore put the possession of the property left by John Payne into the hands of the vicar of East Wickham and the churchwarden., who with three other substantial parishioners were to administer the charity, the churchwarden being empowered to collect the rents. On Tuesday in Easter week each year he was to render in the church a written account of his receipts and disbursements to the other trustees.

From 1688 onwards leases were granted to various tenants; until 1787 the rent was £12.12s. per annum, and in 1818 Thomas Strong of Welling (of whom more later) had it for £54. He also obtained the lease of a plot of land in the parish of Bexley granted to the vicar and churchwarden of East Wickham by the enclosure award when Bexley Heath was being parcelled out. This rectangular plot lay on the south side of the main road now known as the Broadway, at its junction with the modern Townley Road, on a site now partly occupied by the National Westminster Bank. A photograph taken between the two World Wars shows a short terrace of brick cottages at that point known locally as Payne's Charity.

Another local charity was founded by George Hamp who died in 1659, aged 64, and left £5 to form a fund for the relief of the poor of East Wickham. His tomb, 'much sunk in the ground', could be seen in the last century not far from the south entrance of the old church.[31]

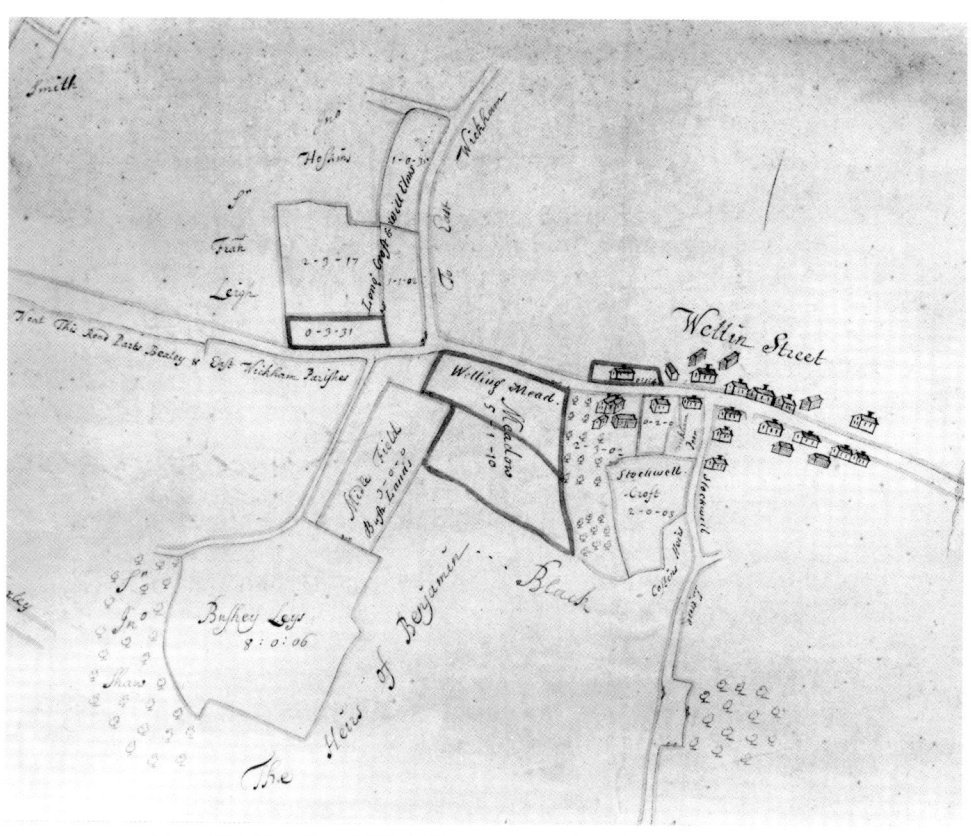

Map of Welling dated 1710. Now in possession of Bexley Local Studies Centre.

Danson

'Dansington' was the medieval name for the manor or estate later known as Danson, lying on the south side of Welling, extending eastward to the approximate line of the present Danson Road, and southward to Blendon and Black Fen. In the reign of Elizabeth I it belonged to Matthew the son of Archbishop Parker and later to his other son, John. An estate map of 1684 showed 'Arleys Wood' covering the slope north of the present lake which did not then exist, though a small stream flowed through the valley, with the old manor house beside it close to Danson Road.

A great deal of the area was then covered in woodland stretching from Danson Road to Danson Lane in Welling, while Arleys Wood and Home Springs Wood together reached from the Dover Road to Blackfen.

In 1698 Danson became the property of John Styleman, a director of the East India Company, who on his death in 1734 left property for the endowment of twelve almshouses which still stand in Bexley village and bear the date 1755. Styleman's widow leased the estate to Colonel John Selwyn, who had been *aide-de-camp* to the Duke of Marlborough, and who lived at Danson until his death in 1751. Soon after this, Danson was purchased by (later Sir) John Boyd, a wealthy London merchant who set about transforming the place into a gentleman's country seat. The existing mansion was designed for him by Sir Robert Taylor and the grounds were laid out probably under the influence of 'Capability' Brown, the foremost landscape gardener of the day. At that time the lake was created by damming the stream at a point close to Danson Road.

Later owners of the property were John Johnson who bought it in 1805, and Alfred Bean after whom Bean Road is named. He was a civil engineer and a great benefactor to the neighbourhood. At Welling he provided an iron church and also a school before his death in 1891. His widow eventually parted with the estate in 1924 to the Urban District Council of Bexley for use as a public recreation ground, a function it still fulfils[32].

The eighteenth century

Edward Hasted, in his *History of Kent* (1797), described East Wickham as possessing seven hundred acres of land and thirty-four houses. Elsewhere it was recorded that in 1796 there were about twenty houses on one side of the highway at Welling.[33]

In his *Bexley Heath and Welling* (1910), the Rev. F.de P. Castells noted the frequent occasions mentioned by John Wesley in his journal of visits to Welling. On his preaching tours, to which he devoted many years of his long life, he passed often through the hamlet, and in 1753 he recorded that he rested there for an hour on account of sickness. Between then and 1766 he referred to being in Welling on eight occasions, when he preached, probably in the open air, to a congregation. When he was sixty-eight he addressed a larger crowd than he had known there for many years, apparently with great effect. Wesley's oratory often evoked dramatic response from his hearers as it did on that occasion in 1771 when a young woman cried out in an expression of penitence that even the

Wickham Lane in the early 1900s, with Foster's School and one of the trams which ran between Woolwich and Dartford.

reassurances of her mother could not pacify. Wesley had reason to know the neighbourhood well on account of his friendship with the Delamotte family of Blendon Hall, and the Rev. Henry Piers, vicar of St. Mary's, Bexley, in whose church his brother, Charles Wesley, preached on a number of occasions.

If Wesley was intent on saving souls, others were concerned with improving the minds of the local children. In 1728, William Foster, a native of the district though later resident in Croydon, left money for the provision of a school where the poor children of East Wickham and Welling could learn reading, writing and arithmetic, the master's salary being £20 a year. A school bearing his name still exists in Wickham Lane but on a site further south than the original building. This stood at the junction of Wickham Lane with what is now Berwick Road, and is marked on the Ordnance Survey map published in the 1860's as 'East Wickham School (Endowed)'. On the 1910 edition of the map it is marked as a Sunday School, the main establishment having been moved to its present premises in 1879. Originally there had been only twenty pupils but due to the increase in population and the implementation of the 1870 Education Act this had expanded to about three hundred. It is interesting to note the continuity of use of the original site for educational purposes, for at the present time the buildings of part of Welling School (Secondary) occupy a position facing Berwick Road a slight distance to the east. When the present Foster's School was built, a stone recording the founder's benefaction was removed from the old school-house and placed on the front wall of the new building with the addition of an inscription recording its removal from its former location.

Hasted remarked that at the east end of the hamlet there was a 'good house', formerly the home of John Denham, son of Peter Denham whose memorial may still be seen on the south wall of St. Nicholas' church at Plumstead. It is there recorded that Peter died in 1736 and that his ancestor was a large benefactor to the 'steeple' of the church. This must refer to the brick tower known to have been erected in 1664 through the efforts of a churchwarden, John Gossage. Peter's son, John, erected the memorial, which mentions his sister,

Elizabeth, who married John Lidgbird who has his own memorial in the church and is thereon described as 'of Shooters Hill'. John Denham's memorial was destroyed when Plumstead church was badly damaged by enemy action in World War II but from an extant photograph it is possible to read that he died on the fifteenth of March 1760, and that he left a widow, Jane, daughter of Thomas Williams of Plaistow in Essex, and an only child, Anne. There is nothing in this epitaph to confirm Castells' statement that he was a military man, a major of the British Army, and Castells gives the name incorrectly as *Denman*. The name of Denham Close has been given to a modern development opposite the football ground on account of the association of that family with Welling.

The position of John Denham's home can be inferred from a statement of Castells that the 'ancient' house was taken over and used by the Rev. Stephen Tucker as a school and that it was nearly opposite the old Guy Earl of Warwick public house. This stood within living memory on the south side of the road about a hundred and thirty yards south-east of the junction with Danson Lane, some way west of the modern public house of the same name, erected to replace it after the demolition of the old building in the 1920s.

East Wickham House was a Georgian residence on the west side of Wickham Street, almost opposite the west end of the modern Darenth Road, the property of successive generations of the Jones family who assumed the position of squires of East Wickham for two centuries. Hasted states that Thomas Jones, who died in 1766, built a house about a quarter of a mile north of East Wickham, near Bostall Heath, and his map shows a house in roughly that position marked 'Wickham Place'. Thomas Jones was Controller of the Laboratory of the Royal Arsenal at Woolwich and married a Miss Pelham by whom he had a son, Colonel Richard Steyner Jones, who died in the West Indies.[34]

On a metal coffin plate in the old St. Michael's church there was an inscription to Master Lewis Thomas Pelham Jones who died in 1763, aged fourteen, and there were two funeral hatchments on the west wall relating to other members of the family, now in the modern church.

The Highways

Until the end of the seventeenth century the usual method of maintaining the highways was to place the legal responsibility on the inhabitants of each parish to repair the roads in their own area. Thus the inhabitants of East Wickham and Bexley were liable for the upkeep of the Dover Road from the foot of Shooters Hill to Crayford. This parochial system proved unsatisfactory for several reasons: the parishioners resented having to repair a road used mainly by travellers from outside the parish and they also lacked the expert skills necessary for proper road construction. During the eighteenth century the custom increased of forming trusts to take over sections of the roads and charge tolls at turnpike gates along the route, the money collected going to to the maintenance of the road. The second road to be

East Wickham House. The Property of Richd. Jones, Esq. From the Epitome of the History of Kent, 1838.

turnpiked in Kent was that from Gravesend to Rochester in 1712. This was much used owing to the fact that travellers to the Continent avoided the dangerous route over Shooters Hill and Bexley Heath by taking a boat down the Thames to Gravesend and proceeding to Dover by road from that point. In 1738, however, the road through Welling was turnpiked and came under the control of the New Cross Turnpike Trust, one of whose gates stood at Crook Log close to the junction with Danson Road. Increased commercial activity resulted in an expansion of road transport in the late eighteenth century and led to a striking growth in the number of coaches and wagons rumbling through Welling.

Highway robbery was one of the hazards passengers had to encounter on the Dover Road, and Shooters Hill and Bexley Heath were notorious danger spots. There are many recorded instances of robberies on this stretch of the road, like that which took place in July 1785 when 'eight gentleman of a respectable character in the City' were returning from a dinner at The Black Bull on Shooters Hill and were held up by two highwaymen who threatened them at pistol point and robbed them of over £20.

The Fanny on the Hill. The beer-house which stood on a site near Wickham Street and the modern White Horse public house.

On another occasion a butcher named Swift was waylaid by three footpads between Welling and Shooters Hill and relieved of his watch and £25. A Captain Dempster returning from Gravesend to London in a coach accompanied by a lady was held up at the foot of the Hill. He put up a stout resistance and fired his pistols at the attackers but they returned his fire and owing to the distress of his female companion he finally parted with his valuables, estimated as worth over £100, and was thereupon allowed to proceed.[35]

In the Welling area there are still persistent legends concerning the supposed activities locally of the notorious Dick Turpin. Most of these appear to have no good historical foundation although Turpin and his companion Rowden were probably active on Blackheath in 1735, having temporarily foresaken their familiar haunts of Hounslow Heath and Barnes Common,[36] and it is not unlikely that at that time they may have extended their activities to Shooters Hill. A former public house at East Wickham, known as The White Horse standing some distance north of its modern successor in Wickham Street, was associated with a local belief that a certain proprietress named Fanny used to signal from that vantage point to highwaymen waiting for coaches coming down the road, and this accounts for the more popular name for the place, the Fanny on the Hill. A short distance away, at the foot of the slope of Bostall Wood, there is a hollow called Turpin's Cave, but this is known to have been only a tunnel running from the side of a chalk pit, no doubt made to obtain material used in conjunction with the brickyards that flourished hereabouts in the nineteenth century. Sand drifting from the slope above has now obscured both pit and tunnel.[37]

The steep gradient of Shooters Hill was a formidable obstacle to laden vehicles especially in bad weather. Charles Dickens describes in his *A Tale of Two Cities* the Dover Mail lumbering up the Hill with the passengers trudging alongside through the mire on a November night in 1775 'not because they had the least relish for walking exercise under the circumstances, but because the hill, and the harness, and the mud, and the mail were all so heavy, that the horses had three times already come to a stop, besides once drawing the coach across the road, with the mutinous intent of taking it back to Blackheath'. At the foot of the Hill, on the Welling side, there was once a notice on the front of a public house advertising that a horse could be hired there to assist vehicles up the slope. This is popularly believed to be the origin of the curious name of a public house now standing on the north side of the road near the parish boundary, the We Anchor in Hope.

The old Toll Gate which stood near the site of the present Crook Log Sports Centre.

The nineteenth century

In 1821 William Cobbett, the outspoken Radical reformer, passed over Shooters Hill and declared the land between Deptford and Dartford to be poor, and the surface ugly by nature. To this unfavourable estimate he added a tirade against the recent enclosure of Bexley Heath which he regarded as an affliction of the poor by depriving them of their ancient rights of common pasture. If Cobbett had halted in Welling he might have met with an inhabitant who shared his concern for improving the conditions of the rural poor. Thomas Strong was at that time one of the principal ratepayers in the parish of Bexley and his business may be inferred from the fact that he was the builder of the new church in Bexley Heath, completed in 1836 and standing on the site of the present War Memorial in Oaklands Road. In the 1830s living was hard for the poor; the Corn Laws kept up the price of bread, wages were low and unemployment common. Strong protested at the cottagers' having to pay rates and at the low wages of twelve to fourteen shillings earned by the labourers. He advocated what would be called nowadays a 'job creation scheme' by which the unemployed should be found work clearing ponds, making roads, planting or removing trees and improving the land.[38]

The New Cross Turnpike Trust put forward a scheme for using the local unemployed in 1816 by proposing the construction of a new road over Shooters Hill. To this end they circulated an enquiry to the local overseers of the poor to discover how many paupers could be supplied to work as labourers. Eleven parishes made their returns, including Bexley, but the records show no response from at least six, including Plumstead and East Wickham. Owing to disputes among the proposers of the undertaking as to how the improvement should be effected, the whole idea was eventually abandoned.[39]

One does not expect a clergyman of the Established Church to be described as a Radical in the early nineteenth century, but the Rev. Stephen Tucker had apparently achieved this reputation. In 1811 he forsook his living of Borden and set up a school in Welling in the Denhams' old house opposite The Guy Earl of Warwick. Despite his reputation for Radicalism, (anyone who expressed sympathy for the underdog might be so labelled in those days) his school was advertised as catering for 'the sons of good families' and was said to offer an excellent classical and mathematical education. Tucker appears to have been a man of wide intellectual interests. It was he who recorded the discovery of the Roman urn in 1829 and the other dug up on his property in 1842 and the occurrence of Roman coins in the next field. One of his sons was Captain William Tucker who commanded H.M.S. Iris, and was drowned in the wreck of the Reliance in 1842 at the age of forty-seven, as recorded on his memorial in the old St. Michael's church.

The old Nag's Head public house which stood on the same site as the later building of the same name.

A large-scale map of East Wickham, made in 1838 by W. Hubbard of Dartford, provides detailed evidence of the appearance of the place in the first half of the century. All the area east of Wickham Lane and north of Welling is shown as farmland, some of the large fields having interesting names such as Hither and Further Longmore, Further Yellow Oak, and Clay Gate. To the west of the Lane were Little Clay Pond Field and Forge Field, among many others. Wickham Lane had only three isolated and widely spaced buildings, including a row of cottages, between the church and the junction with the High Street. Welling itself had no buildings west of that point and on the south side the houses only extended a very short distance west of a site opposite The Nag's Head. This was still an important inn with a yard and stables at the rear, and provided facilities for travellers.

Wickham Street in Victorian times possessed a series of farms and houses commencing at the junction with Wickham Lane, where East Wickham Farm stood with its extensive outbuildings. The old farmhouse, judged to be an eighteenth-century building on its external appearance, is still there, half hidden behind high bushes, and it probably occupies the site of the timber court lodge referred to by Hasted. It is the sole surviving reminder of the vanished rural character of the locality, all the rest having been swept away in the twentieth-century redevelopment. Further on was a row of cottages, standing until 1956, and then came East Wickham House, with a large fishpond at the rear. To the south was Monk's Farm and Dovedale, both close to the side of the road as it wound its way to join the main highway at Shoulder of Mutton Green. This open space was known by that name as early as the middle of the eighteenth century, and it was also called Stroud Green, the former name apparently being a reference to its peculiar shape. Queen's College, Oxford, owned the plot at one time and tried to enclose it in 1866 to the indignation of the local inhabitants who tore down the fences. This led to a protracted law suit and in 1871 the landowners were ordered to allow the Green to remain open. Later, in 1877, it was purchased by the Metropolitan Board of Works to serve as a permanent public amenity.

South side of Welling High Street about 1900. The building just right of centre is the old Guy Earl of Warwick, pulled down in the 1920s.

The East Wickham valley formerly contained extensive deposits of brickearth, most of which has long since been worked out for the manufacture of London stock bricks. The brickyards were flourishing in the second half of the nineteenth century and one continued into the 1930s. They were situated not far from The Foresters public house, at the bottom of the hill below the old church. To obtain chalk to mix with the brickearth, deep shafts were sunk, with galleries running out in various directions at the bottom. At their base these tunnels were nine feet wide, narrowing to three feet at the top, and they were as much as twenty-five feet high. In 1937 dangerous subsidences occurred in the area of Rockcliffe Gardens and Alliance Road, due to the collapse of some of the disused underground workings, and a workman engaged in investigating their extent lost his life in 1939.[40]

As recently as 1958 workings sixty to eighty feet deep were located under the bus garage at the corner of King's Highway and rendered safe by pumping in fuel dust from power stations. This when mixed with water set hard to provide a firm support for the ground above[41].

Towards the end of the nineteenth century there developed a strong popular demand for the railway to link Welling and Bexley Heath with London. The Dartford Loop line through Old Bexley had been opened in 1866 but this was an inconvenient distance away. Local landlords, farmers and shopkeepers all saw the advantages which would come from an increase in population and the enhanced value of their land for building. Market gardeners would be able to send their produce to the capital more expeditiously, a considerable advantage in the case of perishable soft fruit and flowers. At last, in 1895, a line was opened by the South Eastern Railway from Blackheath, through Kidbrooke, Well Hall, Welling and Bexley Heath to Barnehurst. 'Bexleyheath' began to be spelt as one word to encourage comparison by intending

Welling High Street, soon after 1900

residents with Blackheath, then considered a most desirable district. 'Barnehurst' was a name invented for the terminal station from the family name of the local landowner. Few at the time realised how the railway would be responsible for the eventual transformation of the whole area into a dormitory suburb of London, a development which was held back for a while by the 1914-18 War and its immediate economic aftermath.

The nature of these changes is well illustrated by the fate of Westwood Farm. This covered a considerable area of 388 acres to the west of Welling and to the south of the main road, and was in 1895 bisected by the railway line running north-east to south-west. Subsequently when the Rochester Way and Welling Way were constructed, the land was again divided. What then remained was laid out as a housing estate with a multiplicity of roads running in all directions, the names of Westwood Lane and The Green alone preserving the memory of what once had been.

Huts at East Wickham, built in World War I for munition workers employed at Woolwich Arsenal. They were occupied until long after the end of World War II.

Suburbia triumphant

At the commencement of the twentieth century the area around Welling was still predominantly rural in character, many of the inhabitants being engaged in agriculture. But already the area to the north was becoming industrialised, especially near the Thames at Woolwich and Erith. An innovation symptomatic of the urbanisation of the Welling locality was the introduction of electric trams in 1903, running on rails set in the road and drawing their power through an arm connected with an overhead cable. There are many still living who can remember the trams rattling down Bexleyheath Broadway, through the Welling High Street bottleneck, round into Wickham Lane, and down the steep hill at East Wickham on their way to Woolwich. This form of transport served the needs of industrial workers at Woolwich, Erith and Dartford, and the first place was resorted to frequently by housewives on account of the cheap goods sold there in shops and market place.

The trams had replaced the horse-drawn omnibus service from Bexleyheath to Plumstead, which picked up and set down passengers at public houses, like The Nag's Head, along the route or even delivered them to their doors if time and other circumstances permitted.

During the 1914-18 War, the output of arms and munitions from Woolwich Arsenal increased enormously and there was a corresponding expansion of its work force. To accommodate this influx of population a vast settlement of huts, built in tidy rows, was set up at East Wickham south of St. Michael's church and also on the west side of Wickham Lane south of Wickham Street. These were still in use long after the end of the Second World War and have now been replaced by Council housing estates.

Between the Wars, the full effect of the coming of the railway in 1895 was being realised. Private building was responsible for the creation of huge estates of houses priced at figures within the financial capacity of many working people in south London and elsewhere, and within a few years the fields which had once grown fruit and flowers for Covent Garden

Market were buried under concrete, bricks and mortar. In the course of this transformation, nearly all the reminders of the past were swept away in the interest of 'progress'. All the south side of the hamlet of Welling went in the course of road widening made necessary by the greatly increased flow of motorised traffic. On the north side there are still a few relics of the past such as the rebuilt Nag's Head, The Rose & Crown, the eighteenth-century mansard-roofed building (Nos.31-35), and a small number of old premises hidden behind new fronts, like Moat House, disguised at the rear of its petrol station forecourt.

East Wickham House suffered the indignity of having a dog-racing track in its grounds and the house itself, together with a row of cottages in Wickham Street and the former vicarage, are now but memories in the recollection of older inhabitants. Only the old church with the farmhouse and some outbuildings of East Wickham Farm in Wickham Street survive to remind us of the old agrarian hamlet.

As for the environmental amenities, there is little on the credit side to record in the last half century. Hardly any of the modern buildings possess any aesthetic value and the new roads are bordered by endless rows of identical mass-produced houses from which stream every morning the thousands of commuters on their way to the railway station and their work in the big city. Even the three modern Anglican churches are singularly lacking in originality of design although some of their features are worthy of further description.

The first church in Welling was an iron structure built in 1869 at the expense of Alfred Bean of Danson, and it stood north of the site of the later school in Hook Lane.

In 1925 the foundation was laid of St. John's Church in Danson Lane, the architect being Evelyn Hellicar. A brick building in a simplified version of the Perpendicular style, it is a rather sad instance of a twentieth-century church designed in weak imitation of something from a bygone age.

St. Michael's, East Wickham, was built in 1932 to replace the old church considered to be too small for the needs of the locality. The architect was T.F. Ford who designed a brick aisled basilica with an eastern apse, on very traditional lines. The interior is chiefly interesting as containing a number of objects recently removed from the old church when it was taken over by a Greek Orthodox congregation. Mention has already been made of the remounted brasses and the funeral hatchments relating to the Jones family. These latter consist of painted boards bearing the coat of arms of the person commemorated. They were carried in the funeral procession and afterwards displayed on the house of the dead person for several months, after which they were hung in the church. The hatchments in St. Michael's are believed to be those of Ann Sanders, wife of Richard Jones (d.1843), and John Jones, the date of whose death is not stated.[42]

According to a local fable, the old iron coffer now standing near the font was given to the church by Sir John Hawkins and was taken from the Spanish Armada in 1588, for neither of which beliefs is there any historical support. There are other so-called 'Armada' chests in English churches, all constructed on the same principle. A complicated lock is operated through a keyhole in the lid masked by a small plate, while on the front is an ostentatiously mounted fake keyhole, a simple deception so often repeated as to have little effect. Most likely the coffer was used originally for the safe-keeping of the parish registers[43] and was apparently later converted into an alms box by making two slots in the lid. There are also hasps for two padlocks so that the vicar and churchwardens would all need to be present with their separate keys when the box was opened. Many of these iron strong-boxes were made in Germany or Austria in the seventeenth century and imported into this country. Some City livery companies still possess boxes of this type, presumably as part of their goods which survived the Great Fire of 1666.[44]

Bells formerly in the old St. Michael's Church and now in the modern building.

On the front of the west gallery there is mounted the carved and recently repainted Royal Arms of Charles II, and there are three bells taken from the old belfry and now standing on the floor of the north aisle. The oldest bears the name of the founder, John Hodson, and the date 1660, and like the Royal Arms it was probably installed to celebrate the Restoration of the Monarchy in that year. Another bell is uninscribed and the third was cast by S.B. Goslin in 1887, the year of Queen Victoria's Golden Jubilee. A Jacobean-style table once served as a Communion Table in the old church.

A striking recent addition to the interior is a large icon depicting Christ the Divine Word of God in Glory, painted in 1973 by a septuagenarian Russian-born monk of the Orthodox Church, Hieromonk Sophrony. It has been placed behind the altar in the apse and does much to improve the former rather weak focal point of the building.

Icon above the altar of the modern St. Michael's Church, East Wickham.

St. Mary's, on the west side of Shoulder of Mutton Green, was commenced in 1954 and was designed by T.F. Ford. Like St. Michael's, it is a brick structure, with a thin Lombardic tower, the entrance facing the Green and surmounted by a wide arch. On the tympanum are depicted five joyful occasions in the life of the patron saint: the Annunciation, Visition, Birth of Christ, Presentation in the Temple, and the Child Jesus with the Teachers. The stylised figures by Augustus Lunn are produced by cutting into variously coloured layers of plaster, previously applied in successive coats, to reveal the ones required for various parts of the composition. Internally, the shallow sanctuary has over the altar a mural depicting the Ascension of Christ, by Hans Feibusch, and in the transverse arches covering the aisles are painted scenes from the Old Testament, by Clare Dawson. A chapel beside the sanctuary is dedicated to St. Thomas Becket on account of the association of the main road near by with the Canterbury pilgrims in the Middle Ages.

St. Mary's Church, Shoulder-of-Mutton Green, which dates from 1954.

East Wickham and Welling References

1. By Andrews, Dury and Herbert.
2. By Christopher Saxton. *Archaeologia Cantiana* xlix (1938),255-65.
3. *Arch. Cant.* lxxiii (1959),210-11.
4. E. Ekwall, *Dictionary of English Place-Names* (1960).
5. W.de G. Birch, *Cartularium Saxonicum*, I, no.346; and *Arch. Cant.* liv (1941),23-5.
6. I.D. Margary, *Roman Roads in Britain* (1955),45.
7. S.K. Keyes, *Dartford Historical Notes* (1933),624.
8. G.G. Hewlett, *Proc. of the Crayford Manor House Hist. and Arch. Soc.*, iv (1966),12-16.
9. *Arch. Cant.* 1xvi (1953), 77-81.
10. *Arch. Cant.* xvii (1887), 10-11; and 1xviii (1954), 44.
11. J.K. Wallenberg, *The Place-Names of Kent* (1934), 14-15.
12. K.J. Edwards, *Arch. Cant* 1xxxviii (1973), 81-5.
13. P.H. Reaney, *Arch. Cant.* 1xxvi (1961), 59.
14. E. Ekwall, see reference 4.
15. M. Gilling, *Medieval Archaeology* xi (1967), 87-104.
16. E. Ekwall, see reference 4.
17. *Arch Cant*, xli (1929), 207-216.
18. Illustrated in F.R.H. Du Boulay's *Medieval Bexley* (1961) where it is shown in unrestored condition on its original stone, as drawn by T. Fisher in 1809.
19. *Proceedings of the British Archeological Association*, 1845.

20. *The Dictionary of National Biography* (D.N.B.).

21. *D.N.B.*

22. *D.N.B.*, under Charles Leigh. There was a Foxgrave at Beckenham in 1345/6 (*Arch. Cant.* x, 154), and a manor of Foxgrove there in 1776 (*Arch. Cant.* lxxxi, 33).

23. *D.N.B.*

24. F. de P. Castells, *Bexley Heath & Welling* (1910), 34-5.

25. *D.N.B.*

26. Edward Hasted, *History of Kent* (1797).

27. W.K. Jordan, 'Social Institutions in Kent 1480-1660', in *Arch. Cant.* lxxv (1961), 41-2.

28. F.W. Jessup, *Kent History Illustrated* (1966), 41; and *Arch. Cant.* xlvi (1934), 77-96.

29. W.K. Jordan, see reference 27.

30. I am obliged to Mr. H.A. James of the Kent Archaeological Society, who remounted the East Wickham brasses, for this information.

31. Details of Payne's charity taken from a board formerly in the church. A note on Hamp's tomb and charity is inserted by hand in a copy of Lysons' *Environs* in the Local Studies Centre at Hall Place.

32. For fuller details see Mrs. R. Hutcherson's *The History of Danson*, (1984) and Roger Whites article 'Danson Park, Bexley', in *Arch. Cant.* xcviii(1982).

33. D. Lysons, *The Environs of London* (1796).

34. Hasted, see reference 26.

35. Quoted from an unidentified contemporary source in an article by an anonymous contributor to *St. Michael's Parish Magazine* about 1948.

36. D. Barlow, *Dick Turpin and the Gregory Gang* (1973), 224.

37. H. Pearman, *Chelsea Spelaeological Society Research Volume* vi.

38. Castells, see reference 24.

39. F.C. Elliston-Erwood, *Reports of the Woolwich & District Antiquarian Soc.* xxviii (1947).

40. H. Pearman, see reference 37.

41. *Kentish Times*, 28.3.1958.

42. *Arch. Cant.* lxxxi (1966), 93. The date given there for Ann Jones is 1834.

43. The register of baptisms at St. Michael's dated from 1730 and burials from 1715.

44. F. Roe, *Ancient Church Chests and Chairs in the Home Counties Round London* (1929), 36-7.

Index

Addington 19
Arleys Wood 26

Beacons 21
Bean, Alfred 26, 41
Becket, St Thomas 16, 45
Bellegrove 18
Bexley Urban District Council 26
Blendon Hall 28
Boyd, Sir John 26
Brown, Lancelot "Capability" 26
Burnell, Robert 17
Brickyards 37

Celsus, Roman Potter 9
Charter of 814 6
Chaucer, Geoffrey 16
Cobbet, William 34
Crook Log 31

Danson 26
De Bladigdone, John and Maud 13, 14, 15
Delamotte Family 28
Denham, John 28, 29
Dickens, Charles 32
Domesday Book 12
Dover Road 6, 7, 18, 30

East Wickham Farm 36, 41
East Wickham House 29, 30, 41
Enclosures 34
Estwycham 11

"Fanny on the Hill" 31, 32
Farmlands 36
Foster, William 27, 28

Goldie Leigh Property 19
Greek Orthodox Church 14, 42
Guilds 18, 23
Guy, Earl of Warwick 5, 9, 29, 37

Hamp, George	24
Hasted, Edward	19, 27
Hatchments in St Michael's Church	42
Hawkins, Sir John	20, 21, 42
Henry V	16
Highway Robbery	30, 31
Hutments	39, 40
Johnson, John	26
Jones Family	15, 29, 30, 42
Lambarde, William	21
Leigh, Charles	18, 19, 20
Leigh, Frances	18
Leigh, John	19
Lovell, Sir William	17
Metropolitan Board of Works	36
Nag's Head	35
Nate, John	24
Neolithic Stone Axe-Head	6
New Cross Turnpike Trust	30, 31, 33, 34
Noviomagus	7
Olyffe, Sir John	18, 19
Oxford University	36
Payne's Charity	24
Payne, John	22, 23, 24
Payne, William	22, 23
Parker, Archbishop Matthew	26
Peasants' Revolt	16
Piers, Rev Henry	28
Pilgrims' Way	16
Plague	23
Railway	38
Roman Burials	9
Roman Roads	6
Sarcophagus	9
Selwyn, Colonel John	26
Shooter's Hill	21, 31, 34
Shoulder of Mutton Green	5, 36, 45
St John's Church, Danson Lane	41
St Mary's Church, Bexley	23, 28
St Mary's Church, East Wickham	45

St Michael's Church, East Wickham   5, 12-16, 19, 20,
                                     22, 41-43
Strong Boxes 20, 42
Strong, Thomas 24, 34
Styleman, John 26

Taylor, Sir Robert 26
Tithes 20, 21
Trams 40
Tucker, Rev Stephen 29, 34
Turpin, Dick 32

Watling Street 6, 7, 16
"We Anchor in Hope" 33
Wellyngs 10
Welling Secondary School 28
Wesley, John 27
Westwood Farm 39
Wickham Lane 9, 16, 28
World War I 40